NO Turning Back

BY

LOREEN CLOPTON-MASON

To order additional copies of this book, contact:
Xlibris
844-714-8691
www.Xlibris.com
Orders@Xlibris.com

ISBN: Softcover   978-1-4535-1338-5
           EBook   978-1-4771-7499-9

Library of Congress Control Number: 2010908092

Print information available on the last page

Rev. date: 03/23/2023

CONTENTS

NO TURNING BACK

NO TURNING BACK

We are traveling in a vehicle, and end up on a narrow road. As we continue, we notice that there are walls on both sides of the road. We look ahead to see that there is a brightly lit sign, giving us the impression that it is probably a good place to stop, fuel up, get refreshments and use the restrooms. We get closer to the sign, and it reads: FOOD FUEL BEVERAGES NEXT FIVE MILES.

We continue on the narrow road, looking forward to that "NEXT FIVE MILES."

Someone starts describing what kind of refreshments we should all get. Someone else says that we should get a different kind of refreshment. Another person joins in on the discussion to add yet a whole new suggestion as to what refreshment everyone should have. Everyone starts getting louder, causing the driver to yell , "Enough!"

Noticing a brightly lit sign in the rear-view mirror, the driver suddenly hit the brakes, causing everyone to jerk forward. "Look at what you all made me do! We missed our turn!" Someone suggested that we turn around, but the road was too narrow, and the walls made it even more impossible. The driver decided that all we could do was keep going.

Before long, everyone is looking ahead; all eyes are on the road, hoping to see another sign. We soon come upon a sign, but it isn't the type that we are looking for. This sign is a warning about the road ahead being bumpy and uneven. Minutes later, we are being tossed around; some of us put on our seatbelts. The driver slows the vehicle down. Someone asks, "What's going on?" The driver answered,

"The road is uneven, and it has bumps in it; just like the sign said." Astonished, some of us remembered seeing the sign, but didn't read it because it wasn't brightly lit.

The ride is now smoother, so the driver picks up his speed. Nobody notices, but walls are no longer on both sides of the road. We come upon another sign. It reads: SLOW: ROCKS FALLING Immediately following, a sign reads: DEER CROSSING.

Three minutes later, in the near distance, the smallest deer any of us had ever seen was crossing the road. The driver hit the brakes, causing those who were not in seatbelts to tumble around, resulting in bumped heads, busted lips, or bruised knees. Some of us got angry at the thought of such a small creature affecting us in such a huge way. "Where did that deer come from?" someone asked. "How did it get past the walls?" Everyone realizes, at that moment, that the walls are not there.

The driver starts looking back, then checks the rearview mirror to see if he can see the walls that used to be on both sides of the road. While he's concentrating on that mirror, contemplating about when they got past the walls, a big rock rolls into the road. He looks up just in time to see the big rock, and maneuvers the vehicle in order to get back straight on the road.

Once again, everyone is concentrating, looking ahead, preparing for whatever; but watching for, and reading, every sign that comes along . . .

There is more to this story, just as there is more to life. We just have to condition ourselves on paying attention to the signs along the way . . . no matter how small, or how insignificant they may seem at any moment.

Loreen Clopton-Mason

THE BOX

THE BOX

What are we holding on to, and why? Is what we hold on to good, bad, useful, useless? Does what we hold on to help or hurt someone? Are we expecting something from what we hold on to? Do we know?

Late one night, a youth hurriedly tiptoes into the garage and tosses a very pretty stuffed toy into a huge box, while constantly checking and making sure no one is looking. The youth turns around, and with a sigh of relief, rushes back to the bedroom and slides into bed.

Years later, the family prepares for a garage sale. Everyone is working, clearing shelves, cleaning out cabinets, emptying any and everything that could be moved. Finally, all that was left was a huge box. Everyone except the youth, now teenager, starts sorting through the assortment of stuff the box held. Near empty, the huge box was put on its side so that everyone could finish sorting through its contents. Someone pulled out a pretty stuffed toy, and said "Wow! I remember getting this out of the kitchen garbage, a long time ago." Someone else said, "I remember getting it out of the bathroom trash. That's been a while. Actually, I had forgotten about it." Another someone said, "It is too pretty to just throw away. Let's put it up." The teenager walked into the garage, and someone tossed the toy over; saying, "Find somewhere to put this!" Immediately, the family pet snatches the toy from the teen's grasp, ripping it to shreds; stuffing and all. The teen smiled, then reached down and gave the pet a loving pat.

What are we holding on to, and why? Is what we hold on to good, bad, useful, useless? Does what we hold on to help or hurt someone? Are we expecting something from what we hold on to? Do we know?

FAITH

FAITH

-Leaders: Faith . . . Followers: Fate

-Faith.. .It's like I woke up from a multi-year coma, and started opening gifts He left for me . . . He continues to bless me.

-Faith . . . There was a time when my mother could barely speak, but apologized to me as I washed her body. I thank God for the ability to care for her!

-Acknowledging and talking about God had not always been my way of life. Only fairly recently, I inadvertently learned how to really pray. (A 'spirited' person gave me a book that included information about praying.) Our blessings come in many forms.
I have always loved, and have always been a very spiritual person; but found it hard to truly believe in the Father, Son and Holy Spirit. The love in my heart has lead me to see that it (FAITH) was there inside me all along; only now, it has a name. THANK YOU FATHER!

FAITH SWEETENS THE BITTERNESS OF LIFE

THANK YOU FATHER
MY PRAYER

THANK YOU FATHER

Father, I thank You for Your patience. You have allowed me to live life as I choose; to make decisions or choices, some that I knew, or later found were not right, but You gave me the strength to work through circumstances that, now when I look back, seemed impossible to get out of. You blessed me from birth; by surrounding me with a family of people who made it their mission to raise and instill in us the importance of faith and respect. You continue to bless me by allowing me to be able to see life situations as tools to better myself and those who seek an ear to listen, a shoulder to cry on, a heart to truly feel, and does not mind letting people know that they are loved. THANK YOU FATHER!

CHRISTIAN CONVERSATION

CHRISTIAN CONVERSATION

The following is an actual letter to me, with my response .. .

Hey Loreen,
You know what I think about you all the time since I've been thinking and learning way outside the box.
Do you remember the time I came to your house with a friend and we were trying to CONvert you to Christianity?
Well I have to say I'm so sorry for that. I've been studying religions now for the past 4-5 years and see them for what they really are.
I've also been studying our true history and I know who I am and what I am not.
Anyway I remember you not being interested in hearing it and you didn't want anyone talking to your kids about it also. You wanted them to make their own minds up when they got older.
I have a Grand-baby now and from what I've learned I want the vultures to stay away from her and not corrupt her mind.
It is a battle, there is a fight for our minds.
I don't know what path you're own now, but I admire you for taking a stand way back then. I'm doing the same thing now.
Peace & Blessings to you!

Hi there!

My tremendous thanks to you for your kind words, and for reminding me of my "non-religious, anti-Christian" past . Please do not apologize for any of that, for had it not been for people like yourself, I probably would not have found my true spiritual self.
As for my children . . . all (five, including one stepson) have been baptized, and are active in church, and living life by the word. Two are in the military, but always let me know that they never miss chapel.
I truly understand and agree with you about wanting the vultures to stay away from your granddaughter. That is the type of thing I pray for most often . . . our minds and our hearts; especially our children's.
The path I'm on is still pretty much the same, only difference is . . . I pray now.
Thank you for sharing your blessings. I love you.

BUTTERFLY DESCRIPTION

BUTTERFLY DESCRIPTION

Little things make me appreciate bigger things; especially after a particular conversation I once had with a friend .. .

My friend and I were sitting on her front porch, when she asked me about a butterfly. I was astounded of her knowing it was there; her being blind. This left me to describe in detail everything from the designs and shapes of the many markings, locations of the markings, the tiny colorful specks spread around larger markings; different markings, designs and shapes underneath each wing; how wide the wings were, the shape of the wings, the color of the butterfly's body, head and legs, and what color the flower was that it landed on.

When I look back to that moment in my life, it made me realize that until my friend had me to describe that butterfly to her, I was more blind than she. I take very little for granted.

A DOSE OF MEMORIES

A DOSE OF MEMORIES

Death is a part of life . . . Faith gives me the strength to accept that. The following was written by me, Monday, February 22, 2010 at 7:30pm, with corrections...

Lately, I have been feeling down. It never fails; this is the time of year when I suffer most with depression. My days seem longer, with the dread of morning gloom after a sleepless night. I try my best to "get out of this mode" by any means I can think of . . . praying, eating, drinking hot liquids, taking long soaks in the tub . . . These help some, but the deepness of gloom returns soon after.
I am reminded of the reason for this down mode, and why this time of year. On February 25, 2002, a very special four-year-old was laid to rest. My heart aches when I think about the last time I laid eyes on him lying in that little casket. He was born August 30, my sister Della's date of birth . . . I can't help but feel that there is some kind of a symbolic connection. On the morning of my 39th birthday, I said my goodbyes to him.

He came into my life when he was two years old. I was the babysitter for him and his big sister during the summer that year; while their mother worked. Like me, our children grew attached to the two of them. They fit in just like they were their younger brother and sister.

Now, I try to think about some of the earlier, happier times like when he would pitch a fit because he did not want to get out of the bath tub before the "bubbles left," or the times I would have to chase him to save Cookie, my kitten from being 'loved' to death. Those, and many other memories of him are quite medicinal for me . . . better than any prescription.

JUDGE YE NOT

20

LABELING . . . ANOTHER FORM OF JUDGING

Let's say that we have a keg of beer ... .

Someone puts a "tea" label on the outside of the keg . . .

Does that change the beer to tea?

IMPORTANT TO KNOW

IMPORTANT TO KNOW

I have been ridiculed because of me not knowing certain people. I had never been ridiculed because of my not knowing God. Actually, those who find it important for me to know certain people, don't seem to care whether or not I know God.

LETTER TO MY FATHER

FATHER, CAN WE TALK?

Hello! How are you? There are two things that I would like to say to you. First, thanks so much for all the wonderful gifts you have been sending us. Second, thank you for accepting me.

It is hard to believe that you really are my father, because I was always given the impression that my many siblings and I had different fathers. Some of us had me thinking that you never existed, which is something I find quite astounding . . . everyone has to be fathered in order to be in existence. I thought. A number of us made accusations that you simply left, never to return. Still, others said that you were around, but they could not show or tell me where to find you. I am pretty sure that they meant well, but all of that got me so confused.

You are very popular, around here. People talk about you all the time; unfortunately, it is not all good. I am not sure that they realize it, but I was told by some of those same people, that you are very forgiving. Some of them also said that you had only one son, but still claimed that you were everybody's father. Not only that, but it has been said that your son was severely abused by many, and you did nothing about it; instead, I was told, that you forgave those same people responsible for such an act. Is that true? Well, I guess it really doesn't matter because it has been said that your son lives. That's talked about a lot, too.

About the gifts; I just started opening some of mine. They are so wonderful, I can't help but share them. Your gifts are the kind that keep giving. Thank you!

About accepting me; it just feels good to know that I have something to look forward to. Many of my siblings and I have been claimed by some who say that they are our fathers, but they sure don't act fatherly. I look forward to meeting you. My real father.

INSPIRATIONAL QUOTES

INSPIRATIONAL QUOTES

-Words spread like wildfire . . . The Word spreads like the heat of an old shack. It takes time, but eventually it feels good throughout.

-Today is the present, not a present . . . it cannot be returned.

-Question: What is the best way to read the future? Answer: Read the Bible.

-The strong finish the journey; the weak are finished by the journey.

-Are we ready for the storm? More importantly, are we ready for the aftermath?

-When I worked for man, I had no problem taking off every now and then. Now that I work for The Man, I show up proudly, everyday!

-When we respect others, we respect ourselves.

-Respect. Don't leave home without it.

-Prayer sweetens the bitterness in life.

-When we say we don't care what others say about us, we care about what others say about us.

-Are we rooted, or are we waiting to be blown away?

-If it cannot be said at church, it should not be said at home!

-The best insurance to have: FAITH.

-As children, we learn what we live; as adults, we live what we learn.

-As we are traveling in this vehicle of life, are we paying attention to the signs along the way?

Printed in the United States
by Baker & Taylor Publisher Services